Whodunit Math Puzzles

Bill Wise

Illustrated by Lucy Corvino

Sterling Publishing Co., Inc.
New York

For my mother, Roberta B. Wise

Library of Congress Cataloging-in-Publication Data

Wise, Bill 1958–
    Whodunit math puzzles / Bill Wise.
        p. cm.
    Includes index.
    ISBN 0-8069-5986-0
    1. Mathematical recreations. I. Title.
QA95.W68 2000
793.7'4—dc21

00-048263

10 9 8 7 6 5 4 3 2 1

First paperback edition published in 2002 by
Sterling Publishing Company, Inc.
387 Park Avenue South, New York, N.Y. 10016
©2001 by Bill Wise
Distributed in Canada by Sterling Publishing
c/o Canadian Manda Group, One Atlantic Avenue, Suite 105
Toronto, Ontario, Canada M6K 3E7
Distributed in Great Britain and Europe by Chris Lloyd at Orca
Book Services, Stanley House, Fleets Lane, Poole BH15 3AJ,
England.
Distributed in Australia by Capricorn Link (Australia) Pty. Ltd.,
P.O. Box 704, Windsor, NSW 2756 Australia

Sterling ISBN 0-8069-5986-0 Hardcover
              0-8069-8073-7 Paperback

CONTENTS

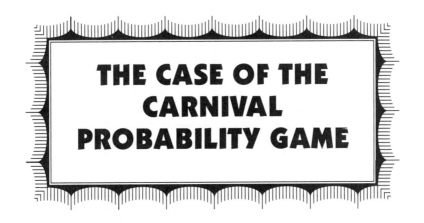

THE CASE OF THE CARNIVAL PROBABILITY GAME

The smells of buttered popcorn, cotton candy, and fried dough filled the air as Midville Police Chief Arthur Smart and his partner, 12-year-old junior detective Cal Q. Leiter, passed through the gates of the 85th annual Midville Fair. The Chief had been asked to participate in the pie-eating contest, and Cal had tagged along to support him.

"You know, it's gonna be difficult to stick to my diet today," said the Chief, eyeing the food stands that lined both sides of the walkway. He stopped in front of Perry's Pizza booth. "Maybe I'll have just a tiny slice of pizza before the contest."

"Do you really think that's a good idea, Chief?"

"Give me one good reason why I shouldn't."

Before Cal could reply, the Chief blurted out, "Hey, look. That's my cousin Norman arguing with that vendor over there."

Cal looked across the way and spotted a short, pudgy man who could pass for the Chief's twin gesturing wildly and stomping up and down. The Chief and Cal rushed over to see what the commotion was all about.

The vendor, a lanky man with long sideburns, stood

behind his counter, shaking his head smugly. "You lost, fair and square," he said, pointing at Cousin Norman.

The Chief patted Norman on the back. "Norman, what's going on here? I've never seen you this angry."

"I'll tell you what's going on here," Norman said through gritted teeth. "A big-time ripoff! This guy here is running some sort of crooked scam. I just can't figure out how he's doing it."

Cal looked up at the sign over the booth. It read: "CHANCES ARE — A GAME OF LUCK. Toss three coins. One head, you win $3. Two heads and the vendor wins. Three heads or no heads, no one wins, and we try again. Cost to play: $2."

"Let me get this straight," said the Chief. "Let's say you play once and win. It cost you $2 to play, and you won $3, so you really made $1. Isn't that right, Cal?"

Cal nodded and began drawing a diagram in his math notebook.

"And if you lose, you lose the $2 you paid to play, right?"

Again Cal nodded.

The vendor gave his side of the story. "Look," he said. "It's twice as hard to get two heads as it is to get one head. That's why it's a fair deal that if I win, I get twice as much as when I lose."

The Chief thought for a moment. "Makes sense to me."

"Wait," screamed Cousin Norman. "I've played this game 48 times. I've won 16 times, he's won 18 times; neither of us won 14 times. I've lost $20 bucks to this schemer. That shouldn't happen, should it?"

"Hey, haven't you heard of a lucky streak?" asked the vendor, smirking.

The Chief picked up the three coins from the counter and carefully examined each of them. "Nothing's wrong with the coins, Norman. Look, I'm sorry you lost, but it appears that this just wasn't your day. That's all."

"It doesn't make sense," said Norman. "Probability says I should have won twice as often as he did and that we should have broken even money-wise, doesn't it?"

Finally, Cal spoke up. "No, it doesn't," he said. "In fact, things pretty much went according to probability." Cal looked up at the Chief. "Chief, your cousin is not correct about probability, but he is correct about one thing: This game is a ripoff. Big time. This vendor has a guaranteed winner with his game."

"Well, that's enough for me," bellowed the Chief. He turned to the vendor. "You, sir, are shutting down and coming downtown with us."

How is this game unfair? What did Cal figure out? *(Solution on page 89.)*

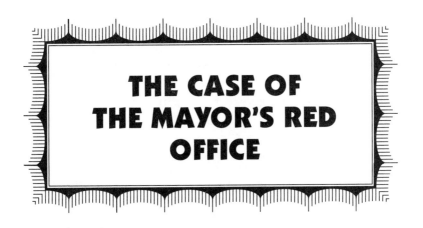

THE CASE OF THE MAYOR'S RED OFFICE

Midville Police Chief Arthur Smart and his 12-year-old sidekick Cal Q. Leiter stood staring in shock at the mayor's office. Everything — the ceiling, the walls, the carpet, the furniture — had been slopped with bright red paint. It was an unbelievable scene.

Just then, the honorable Midville mayor, Linda Fuller, stormed into the room. "We must find out who did this," she said, turning to the Chief. "I want you to make finding this vandal your number-one priority, Chief."

"I've already got two of my best officers on this," replied the Chief.

Cal took out his trusty notebook. "When did this happen, Chief?"

"This morning between 10:30 and 11:00. The entire staff was with the mayor at a dedication."

Suddenly, the door swung open, and two Midville police officers arrived with three people. Two of the civilians, a man and a woman, wore painting overalls which just happened to be covered with red paint. The third person, a gray-haired man in a three-piece suit, stood beside the painters, shaking his head in disbelief.

"Chief," said Officer Beth Belisle, "we have some definite leads on this case." The officer pointed to the gray-haired man and said, "This is Ned Woodland, owner of Woodland Painting. The other two are, obviously, painters. They work for Mr. Woodland."

"What's the scoop here?" asked the Chief.

Mr. Woodland spoke up. "These officers spotted my painters leaving work today and brought them in. I know they look like logical suspects because of the red paint, but they didn't do it. There's no way. "

Cal was curious. "Were you with them all morning, sir?"

"Let me explain," said Mr. Woodland. "Harry and Sue here are painting rooms in a hotel downtown. The hotel has 50 identical rooms, and they've done about half of them so far. Sometimes they work alone and sometimes together. I've timed them together many times and it takes them 2 hours as partners to do a room. I've also timed Sue when she's done a room alone, and it consistently takes her 6 hours. I've never timed Harry alone."

"That doesn't answer the kid's question," said the Chief.

"O.K.," said Mr. Woodland. "I was with Sue virtually the entire morning, so I'm her alibi. I checked in on Harry at 7:00 a.m. when he was starting, and again at

11:15 when he had just finished. It takes 30 minutes to get to the mayor's office from the hotel. That's a one-hour round trip. It must have taken 10 to 15 minutes to vandalize this office. That would leave Harry three hours to paint that room back at the hotel. I don't think he's capable of doing that — it takes Harry and Sue two hours together."

The Chief frowned. "Well, we'll never know if he's capable, will we? We don't have enough information to solve the math problem."

Just then the mayor yelled, "Aha!" She pointed to Harry. "I knew you looked familiar! You used to work for our town. I fired you last year for skipping work too many times. I'll bet you did this to get revenge."

"Sorry, Mayor, that's not proof," said the Chief. "And, remember, we don't have enough math info to solve this case."

Cal held up his notebook. "Yes, Chief, we DO have enough information. Not only did Harry have motive, but he also had the time. And here's the math to prove it."

How did Cal figure that Harry had time to commit this act of vandalism? (HINT: Use the least common multiple to help you figure this out.) *Solution on page 89.*

THE CASE OF THE HIT-AND-RUN TAXI DRIVER

"This is going to be a bear of a case to solve," said Midville Police Chief Arthur Smart, swabbing the perspiration from his forehead with a damp handkerchief. "We can't talk to the victim, and there were no witnesses."

"I know, Chief," said 12-year-old junior detective Cal Q. Leiter. "But you can never underestimate the power of mathematics when it comes to solving problems. As the great mathematician Pythagoras once said, 'Number is the origin of all things, and the law of number is the key that unlocks the secrets of the universe.'"

It was a hot, humid, stifling day in late August. Chief Smart and Cal were standing in front of an old brick house on Mountain Road, about three miles from Midville Center. The house was owned by a man named Peter Wheeler.

Earlier in the day Wheeler had been found unconscious on the side of the road near his driveway. He had been beaten and robbed. Wheeler had written the words "TAXI DRIVER" in the soft shoulder sand on the side of the road before he had passed out. The only other clue was a $3.90 taxi receipt for a 3.3 mile trip that police officers had found on the ground near Mr. Wheeler.

"Poor guy," said Chief Smart, as he cased the grounds for more clues. "I hope he regains consciousness soon. The doctors are hopeful that he'll come out of it in a day or so."

"But by then the criminal could be long gone," said Cal.

The Chief frowned. "That's why we need to solve this case, pronto. But where do we even begin? Except for the message in the sand and the taxi receipt, we've come up empty in the clues department."

"Chief, how many taxis do we have in Midville?" asked Cal.

"Just three," answered the Chief, mopping his sweaty brow. "And I have an info report on each one, back in the cruiser."

While Chief Smart went to the patrol car to get the

official report, Cal removed a math notebook from his tattered backpack. He recorded the facts he knew thus far.

Seconds later the Chief returned, holding a manila folder in his right hand and two bottles of water in his left. He tossed Cal one of the bottles.

"As I said, there are three taxis: Freddy's Taxi, Smalltown Taxi, and ASAP Taxi." The Chief then opened the manila folder and read off the facts from the report. "Freddy's taxi driver is Freddy Yost. He charges an initial rate of $1 for the first half-mile and then 10 cents for each additional tenth of a mile. Smalltown Taxi is driven by Mary Jill Haverhill. She charges an initial rate of $1.10 for the first half-mile and then 10 cents for each additional tenth of a mile. And ASAP Taxi is really Tony Sadowski. He charges an initial rate of $.50 for the first two-tenths of a mile and then 10 cents for each additional tenth of a mile."

The Chief looked up from the report and sighed. "I know this information should help somehow. But I don't know where we begin when it comes to working with all of these numbers." The Chief stopped talking and took a big gulp of water. "I guess we're going to have to use the old guess-and-check method and hope we stumble upon some sort of a clue."

By this time, Cal had finished writing the facts in his notebook. Working diligently, he spent the next few minutes organizing the information.

The Chief pointed to the car. "Let's go back to the office and try to —"

"Hold on, Chief," interrupted Cal. "We've got some-place we need to go first." He finished drinking his bottled water. "We have a suspect to question, a certain taxi driver who almost got away with beating and robbing a person."

"How in the world did you make sense out of all of those numbers?" asked an astonished Chief Smart.

"By organizing the facts, Chief," answered Cal. "As I told you earlier, you have to believe in old Mr. Pythagoras. Numbers truly are the keys that unlock the secrets of the universe."

How did Cal know which taxi driver attacked Mr. Wheeler? *(Solution on page 88.)*

THE CASE OF
THE CHIEF'S
OLD PARTNER

Cal Q. Leiter looked up from his book, *The History of Irrational Numbers,* and saw Becky Smart, the Chief's daughter, standing in the doorway of Chief Smart's office.

"This is a fascinating book," said Cal. "You know, once I start reading this stuff, I can't seem to stop."

"I know, Cal; I know," said Becky. "But if you want my help with the research paper that's due tomorrow, we need to go to the library."

"Oh, all right," said Cal. He jammed the book into a tattered backpack and reached for his coat.

Suddenly, Chief Smart charged through the door. "Kids, I need your help," he said, ushering Cal and Becky out the door. "Hurry, hurry. The patrol car is parked out front."

Riding in the Chief's cruiser, Cal and Becky sat patiently, waiting for the Chief to tell them where they were going. But the Chief said nothing. He drove silently, his eyes riveted to the road.

After a few minutes had passed, Becky spoke up. "Dad, what's going on here? You come racing into

your office and whisk us away, practically shoving us down the stairs and into your patrol car; and then you say absolutely nothing. What gives?"

The Chief managed a feeble smile. "I'm sorry, Beck. I guess my mind is on poor old Wally Wilkerson."

"Who?"

"My old partner, Wally Wilkerson." The Chief pointed to a faded photograph that was attached to the sun visor on the passenger's side. "Wally's in the first row, the third one from the left. He was a veteran cop when I was a rookie. Wally retired from the force about 15 years ago, and now he works as a security guard at that ritzy high-rise building over in Mercer."

"Is he in some sort of trouble?" asked Cal.

The Chief nodded. "He sure is. Two hundred thousand dollars were stolen from the security box in the vault that Wally was supposed to be guarding. Of course, everybody is furious with Wally."

When the three friends arrived at the high-rise building in Mercer, they found Mr. Wilkerson in the ground floor lobby, surrounded by a crowd of people.

"Like I told you earlier, Judkins, the elevator man, phoned me and told me there was trouble in the basement," said old Mr. Wilkerson. "When I stepped off the elevator there, I got clubbed on the head from behind."

"Oh come on, old-timer, you're just trying to cover up for falling asleep on the job," said a short, bearded man who was wearing an elevator usher's suit. "I never called you. Besides, I've seen you asleep on the job twice this past week."

Mr. Wilkerson shook his fist at the elevator operator. "Darn you, Judkins, that's a lie, and you know it."

Chief Smart wove his way through the crowd and approached Wally Wilkerson. "Come on, Wally," the Chief said calmly. "Let's go somewhere to talk."

A few minutes later, Cal, Becky, the Chief, and Mr. Wilkerson were sitting on a bench in the ground floor lobby.

"I'll stake my reputation as an ex-cop that Judkins did it," said Mr. Wilkerson. "That creep has been staking out the vault for the past two weeks and in the meantime has been trying to make me look bad whenever he's had the opportunity. I'm sure it was all part of his plan to plant in people's minds that I was an incompetent old goof and then conk me over the noggin so he could get to the vault."

Mr. Wilkerson handed the three detectives the robbery report. "Judkins says that he was working in his elevator when the money was stolen," he said, shaking his head. "But nobody remembers seeing him at the elevator that he claims to have been in."

After listening to Mr. Wilkerson, the detectives met Judkins at the elevator he operated. A slick talker, Judkins maintained that he was working his shift as elevator usher when the theft took place.

"I've got other people's statements here, Judkins," said the Chief, holding up the copy of the police report. "And no one recalls seeing you working this elevator between 9:00 and 9:15."

"That's because no one ever remembers the elevator usher." Judkins reached for a worksheet that was hanging on the elevator wall. "Take a look at this," he crowed. "I arrived at 9:00 a.m., taking my station at the ground floor. The robbery occurred at 9:10. This is a running tally of what I did during the time the robbery took place. You can clearly see that with all of this going up and down and down and up, I was busy working here in this elevator at 9:10."

The Chief grabbed the tally sheet and read the following: "+6, – 4, +5, – 8, +2, +4, –7, +2, +2, – 7, +5, +3, – 5, +3, +2, +7, – 4, + 8, – 2, –3, + 4, – 4, +9, – 8, +5." He then gave the tally sheet to Cal and Becky. "There's more, too. Certainly enough to keep Mr. Judkins busy all morning, just like he said."

"Mr. Judkins," said Becky, looking at the elevator panel which housed the control buttons. "How many floors are there in this building?"

Judkins' eyes narrowed suspiciously. "There's a basement, a ground floor, and then floors 1 through 15."

Cal fumbled for his math notebook and began calculating. After a few minutes, he was finished. He tore out the piece of paper and handed it to the Chief.

The Chief scratched his head. "What does all of this mean?"

"It means Mr. Judkins has been lying," said Cal. "He must have hurriedly written this false tally report after robbing the vault. If you look closely, you'll see that in his rush to provide an alibi, Mr. Judkins made a huge mistake."

What was Judkins' mistake? *(Solution on page 87.)*

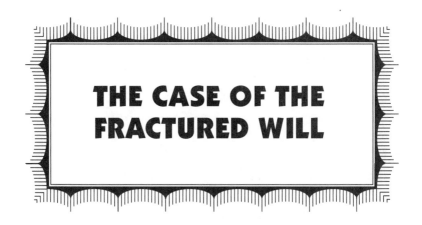

THE CASE OF THE FRACTURED WILL

Ichobod M. Rich, senior partner in Midville's prestigious law firm of Moore, Moore and Rich, tilted back in his plush leather chair and wrinkled his brow. "This is a most unusual situation, gentlemen," he said to Police Chief Arthur Smart and junior detective Cal Q. Leiter. "My clients, Marge and Henry Gessler, have a substantial amount of money coming to them, but due to extenuating circumstances, we can't figure out how much."

"Hmmmmm, Gessler," the Chief said. "That name rings a bell."

"It should," replied Mr. Rich. "Gertrude Gessler was one of the richest people that Midville has ever known. She lived in town about forty years ago."

The Chief leaned forward. "Has there been a crime committed here, Mr. Rich?"

"Yes," Rich answered. "There has been a crime committed. A crime of money. A crime of math. And I've heard that you two specialize in figuring out math problems." He pointed at Cal. "In fact, folks in town say that this kid here is practically a mathematical wizard."

"So what's the problem?" asked the Chief.

"It's rather complicated." Mr. Rich dug into a gold-plated leather briefcase and pulled out a yellowed piece of paper. The paper was worn and tattered. "This document could — let me correct myself — *should* make my clients very wealthy people. Last week, Henry and Marge Gessler discovered the document in the bottom of an old trunk in their basement. The trunk was given to Henry by Gertrude Gessler shortly before Gertrude passed away some forty years ago."

The Chief reached for the tattered piece of paper and read it aloud. "I, Gertrude Gessler, have decided to leave my entire fortune — down to the last dollar — to my four nephews. Some of my nephews were more helpful than others, so I will distribute the money accordingly. Here is the manner in which my money is to be allotted: one-half of the money will go to Henry Gessler, then one-half of what is left from that will go to Jonathon Gessler, then one-third of what is left from that will go to Edward Gessler, and the remaining $800,000 will go to Montgomery Gessler. My skilled team of accountants assures me this works out perfectly, and it is what I want done."

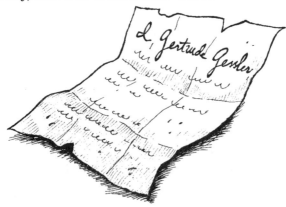

"This will is over forty years old," said Cal. "Wasn't it put into effect back then?"

Mr. Rich shook his head. "That's the problem. It wasn't enacted back when it should have been. Like I said, Henry and Marge just recently found this will. You see, Priscilla Pennypacker, one of Gertrude's lawyers, stole this will and hid it in the trunk forty years ago and then forged a fake will that left Gertrude's fortune to her."

The Chief whistled. "Wow," he said. "So for all of these years, Priscilla Pennypacker has had all of that money and the four nephews never got their hands on a single dime."

"That's correct," said Rich. "What we need to do now is to right this horrible wrong and distribute the money to the nephews in the increments that Gertrude had originally wished."

"That shouldn't be any problem," said Chief Smart. "Let's just go back and look at the original records of what old Pennypacker received from the Gessler estate forty years ago."

Ichobod Rich frowned. "Unfortunately, those records have long been destroyed."

"Did you talk to Priscilla Pennypacker?" asked the Chief. "We can get the original amount from her and divide it among the four nephews now. Obviously, the nephews have lost a lot of dividends that they could have accumulated over all of these years, but at least they'll get what they originally should have gotten."

"I agree," said Mr. Rich. "That is the only route to go. And I did talk to Pennypacker's big-city lawyers."

"And?"

Mr. Rich frowned again. "The lawyers said that

although Priscilla Pennypacker is a multimillionaire now, she claims that she received less than $2,000,000 from Gertrude's will. And that's all she says she is going to turn over to the four nephews — $2,000,000. Henry Gessler, as well as the other Gessler nephews are crying foul. They say that Gertrude was worth millions more than that and that old lady Pennypacker is lying through her false teeth."

"Clearly," said the Chief, "the difference between dividing $2,000,000 out as compared to millions is nothing to sneeze at. The four nephews stand to lose a ton of money if we can't figure out exactly how much Gertrude was worth and prove it." He turned to Cal. "Well, Calvin, what do you think? It doesn't seem like we have enough information to solve this problem. Can we figure out how much money old Gertrude had when she wrote out her will?"

At first Cal didn't answer. He was too busy writing calculations in his notebook.

"Cal?"

"Hold on a few seconds, Chief," he said, finishing his last calculation. He looked up from his work and handed Ichobod Rich the notebook. "Here you go, sir."

Mr. Rich gazed at the notebook and beamed. "You mean, you figured it out? This is how much? Are you positive? Can you prove it?"

Cal nodded. "Absolutely, positively positive. I can guarantee that this math will hold up in a court of law."

"I don't know how you did it," Mr. Rich said to Cal, "but my clients are going to be very, very happy."

How much money did Gertrude Gessler leave to divide among her four nephews? *(Solution on page 90.)*

THE CASE OF THE QUESTIONABLE CARPET DEALER

"After we're done at the carpet store, remind me to stop at the bakery across the street," said Police Chief Arthur Smart.

The Chief's partner, 12-year-old Cal Q. Leiter, laughed. "That's not part of your new diet, Chief," he said. "What's the matter, the garden salad you had for lunch didn't fill you up?"

"That salad wouldn't have filled up a hamster," replied the Chief. "Besides, I'm getting tired of eating salads. That's three days in a row that my wife has packed a small salad for my lunch."

The Chief steered the patrol car to the curb and parked in front of a store called The Magic Carpet. With notebook in hand, Cal hopped out of the car. The Chief, a step behind Cal, was still eyeing the bakery as the two friends approached The Magic Carpet. Just then, a tall redheaded lady sprinted out the store's front door.

"Well, if it isn't Shady Sadee Simmons," said the Chief. "What are you doing here?"

Shady snorted. "I own this store," she said. "I'm the one who phoned in the robbery."

"Trying to make an honest living for once — eh, Shady?"

"Yes, I am," she responded. "But wouldn't you know it. In a bit of irony, I've been a victim of a crime."

The Chief eyed Shady suspiciously. "How's that?"

"Well," Shady began, "I opened this store just last week — with money I earned from an investment — and I was robbed this morning."

The Chief rolled his eyes. "Right, Shady, an investment. That's a funny one."

"I've turned over a new leaf, Chief," she said. "And stop calling me Shady."

Cal spoke up. "Could you tell us what happened, Ms. Simmons?"

Shady smiled. "Yes, young man, I can," she said. " I had five of my best area rugs stolen. They were handmade highly crafted products worth $1000 each."

"Where were they stolen from?" asked Cal.

Shady gestured to the store. "Out back, in the warehouse." She started toward the door. "Come on, I'll take you there."

Cal and the Chief followed Sadee Simmons through the store, out the back door, and into the warehouse.

Once inside the warehouse, the Chief whispered to Cal, "I don't trust her for one second. I'll bet you dollars to doughnuts that she's been up to no good."

"Maybe she has changed, Chief. Let's see what this is all about."

As Sadee talked to the Chief, Cal looked around the tiny warehouse and saw it was empty. "Where were the carpets, Ms. Simmons?"

"All five were on the floor, stretched out. I had unrolled them and set them out to be vacuumed and shampooed."

"Were all of these rugs the same size?" asked Cal.

"Yes."

The Chief cut in. "This is an awfully small warehouse, Shady — I mean, Sadee. What are the dimensions?"

"It's 40 feet by 50 feet, 2000 square feet."

Cal jotted the information in his notebook. "You said all of the rugs were the same size. What size would that be?"

"Each was 20 feet by 18 feet."

The Chief fished a calculator out of his coat pocket and did a few calculations. "20 times 18 equals 360, and 360 times 5 equals 1800. So, the five carpets have a total of 1800 square feet. That means there's plenty of room for the carpets to fit."

"Yes," said Sadee. "Your figures are correct, Chief. I had plenty of room for the carpets. In fact, there were a couple of feet between any two carpets."

"Well, Sadee, I'll put my best officers on this," said the Chief.

Cal grabbed the Chief by his coat sleeve. "Wait a second, Chief. I've just drawn a picture that you need to see. Things are not what they might seem as far as the math of this matter is concerned."

The Chief snatched the paper from Cal and took a look. "Well, I'll be," he said, shaking his head. "Look's like Sadee is still Shady after all." The Chief turned to Sadee. "Nice try, Shady. You almost pulled this one off. But it's off to police headquarters for you."

What did Cal figure out by drawing a picture?

(Solution on page 92.)

THE CASE OF
THE MISSING
COUNTRY CLUB FUNDS

It was 7:00 o'clock on Saturday morning. Young Cal Q. Leiter looked out the clubhouse window at the first tee, where a dozen or so golfers were waiting to tee off. Cal yawned and stretched. He was half asleep. The 10-minute ride from his house to the Whispering Pines Country Club had done little to wake him up.

Cal looked over at his friend, Police Chief Smart, and chuckled. The Chief was ordering coffee, doughnuts, and muffins at the clubhouse restaurant. He had told Cal that his low-fat diet was being put on hold for just this one day.

After the Chief paid for his food, a large, gray-haired man approached him, and the two walked over to where Cal was standing. The Chief spoke first. "Cal, this is Mr. Dean, president of Whispering Pines Country Club."

Cal shook Mr. Dean's hand. "Nice to meet you, sir."

Mr. Dean cleared his throat. "Well, gentlemen, we at Whispering Pines have a problem of great magnitude. I believe that our golf association treasurer, Lenny Ray, may have embezzled Whispering Pines money."

"Got any proof?" asked the Chief.

Mr. Dean frowned. "Not anything tangible," he said. "But when a man of modest income all of a sudden goes out and buys an expensive sports car and a whole new wardrobe and then tells you that the golf association funds have run dry.... Well, it gets one thinking."

"How much was in the treasury?" asked Cal.

Mr. Dean frowned again. "I don't know," he said sadly. "Lenny claimed the computer crashed after he had distributed funds to the chairpeople of the various club committees. He says he can't remember how much was in there before he distributed the money."

"Where are the chairpeople of each of those committees now?" inquired Cal.

"In the meeting room, out back," answered Mr. Dean. "I called all of them in this morning, so they could talk with you."

Cal and the Chief questioned each chairperson. When they were through, they met with Mr. Dean in his office.

"Well, that wasn't any help," said the Chief, shaking his head. "Lenny Ray told the chairpeople what fraction of the total treasury fund they were given, but without knowing how much money was in the treasury beforehand, we're at a dead end."

"Drat," Mr. Dean sighed. "Well, you gave it your best, gentlemen. Thank you for trying."

Cal looked up from his math notebook. "Hold on, Mr. Dean," he said, smiling. "I think we can help you."

"But we don't know how much money was originally in the treasury," said the Chief, looking at Cal blankly.

Cal handed his notebook to the Chief.

The Chief read the notes aloud. "Chairpersons' report of treasury budget. The treasury funds were

allocated in the following manner: lawn mowing equipment ($1/4$); course supplies ($1/5$); pro shop clothes ($1/20$); restaurant supplies ($1/18$); employee salaries ($3/10$)."

Chief Smart scratched his head and handed the notebook back to Cal. "What does all of this tell you, Cal?"

"We can't figure out how *much* Lenny Ray embezzled," said Cal, as he finished up his calculations. "But we can prove that he *did* embezzle. It's right there in the numbers."

How did Cal figure out that there was money missing from the treasury? *(Solution on page 93.)*

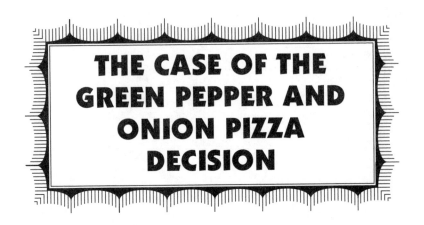

THE CASE OF THE GREEN PEPPER AND ONION PIZZA DECISION

"Well, Cal, what are you going to have?" asked Midville Police Chief Arthur Smart.

Cal Q. Leiter looked up from his menu and shrugged. "I don't know, Chief; everything looks great."

Cal and the Chief were sitting in a booth at Joyce's Pizza Palace with Midville mayor Linda Fuller and Midville town manager Diane Stallworth. The Chief and Cal had just wrapped up an important case, and the mayor and town manager had invited them to lunch. The mayor said it was the town's treat.

At this moment, the smell of pizza wafted through the tiny restaurant, and Cal was getting hungrier by the second. He cleared his throat, hoping the Chief would catch the hint.

"What about you two?" the Chief asked, waving his menu toward the mayor and town manager.

"I like green pepper and onion," answered Mayor Fuller.

"Sounds good to me," echoed Town Manager Stallworth.

The Chief broke into a big grin. "That's my favorite topping, too."

"Well, let's make it unanimous," said Cal. "Green pepper and onion."

The Chief put on his reading glasses and looked at the menu. "It costs $5.50 for a 12-inch pizza and $11 for a 24-inch pizza." He paused. "Should we order four small or two large?"

"Chief, what does it mean when it says a pizza is a 12-inch or 24-inch pizza?" asked Cal.

"That's the distance across the pizza."

"You mean the diameter, Chief?"

"Yes." The Chief nodded. "If you want to get technical, the diameter."

Cal reached for a napkin and began scribbling calculations.

Just then, the waiter approached the booth. "Have you made your decisions?"

"Everyone wants green pepper and onion pizza," said the Chief. "But we haven't decided whether we should get four 12-inch pizzas or two 24's."

"It doesn't matter," said the waiter, his voice ring-

ing with confidence. "A 12-inch pizza costs $5.50. A 24-inch pizza costs $11. Seeing how 24 is double 12 and $11 is double $5.50, it's going to cost the same and you're going to get the same amount of pizza either way. I recommend four small, so you can each have your own pizza."

"We'll take your advice, sir," said the Chief.

"Wait just a second," said Cal, holding up the napkin. "It does make a difference whether we order two large or four small. And since the bill is the town's treat, I think we should make sure we spend the money wisely."

"What are you talking about?" said the Chief, yanking the napkin out of Cal's hand. He looked at Cal's calculations. "He's right. The kid is right again."

The Chief looked at the waiter. "We've changed our minds," he said. "We'll go with two large green pepper and onion pizzas."

"Actually, Chief, we need to order just ONE large pizza," said Cal. "With one large, we'll get the same amount as we would if we ordered four small, and we'll save the town $11."

Upon hearing that statement, the Chief, the mayor, and the town manager all turned to Cal in disbelief.

"Even though it seems impossible, it's true," said Cal. "With the diameters of these particular pizzas, one large pizza has the same area as the combined areas of four small pizzas. And I can prove it by using pi on these pizza pies."

What did Cal figure out? How can one large pie possibly be the same amount of pizza as 4 small? *(Solution on page 90.)*

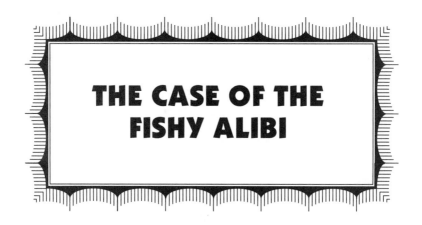

THE CASE OF THE FISHY ALIBI

Junior detective Cal Q. Leiter tried on his new baseball glove for about the zillionth time. Chief Smart had given the mitt to Cal as a token of his appreciation for the many cases that Cal had helped him solve.

"I'll bet you'll make some terrific catches now," said Chief Smart.

Cal nodded. "This will certainly help," he replied. "My old glove was falling apart, and I had been using duct tape to hold it together."

"You know, my daughter Becky is a darn good softball player," said the Chief.

"And a pretty good catch, too. Ha, ha. Get it? Pretty good catch. After we solve this case, you ought to drop by and pay her a visit."

Cal blushed. He had a crush on Becky, and the Chief liked to tease him about it. "Yeah, maybe later. But we have work to do first."

Cal and the Chief were on their way to the Midville wharf. The day before at 4:00 p.m. a man had robbed Roland's Fish and Chips restaurant, a cheap eatery located on the pier. The suspect was Frank G. Roy. Cal and the Chief had an appointment to meet Mr. Roy at the site of the crime.

When Cal and the Chief arrived at the restaurant, they were greeted by the strong smell of fresh fish. The suspect, Mr. Roy, was sitting at a table, a plate of fried shrimp in front of him.

"I'm innocent, I tell you," said Frank G. Roy. "And I have two witnesses to prove it."

"Who?" asked the Chief.

Frank pointed to two men sitting at the bar. "Those two, Malcolm Morrissette and Paddy Smith," he said. "Yesterday at 4:00, the three of us were working on Paddy's boat at a dock that's about a mile from this wharf."

Upon hearing their names, Malcolm Morrissette and Paddy Smith got up from their seats and strolled over to Roy's table.

When questioned, both men supported Frank's story. "You see, all three of us have our own boats and run our own island touring services," said Malcolm.

"Yeah," said Paddy, his lips curling up into a sarcastic grin. "When one of us needs help, the other two always come through."

"Tell us about your touring services," said Cal. He grabbed a notebook from his tattered backpack.

"Well," said Frank. "We all left the pier yesterday morning at 8 a.m. That's the time we depart each morning."

"Right," said Paddy. "I did my regular route, with each round trip being three hours."

"And I did my regular route," said Malcolm. "That's 6 hours each round trip."

"And mine is four hours," added Frank.

Cal jotted down the numbers in his math notebook. "Are your trips nonstop?" he asked. "In other words, as soon as you drop tourists off, do you pick up the new ones?"

"That's correct," answered Paddy. "And we are always right on schedule each time we go out. I always take exactly 3 hours, Malcolm 6 hours, and Frank 4."

"We do that from 8 a.m. until 8 p.m. every day," said Frank.

"I suppose we could try to find some of the passengers these three characters had yesterday," the Chief spoke up. "Then we could find out if they really were working on a boat together at 4 p.m."

Cal smiled. "No need to do that, Chief. Frank's alibi

is all wet. They were right about one thing, though. When one of them needs help, they other two do come through — even if it means lying. These three gentlemen should be arrested."

How did Cal know they were lying? What was wrong with the alibi? *(Solution on page 91.)*

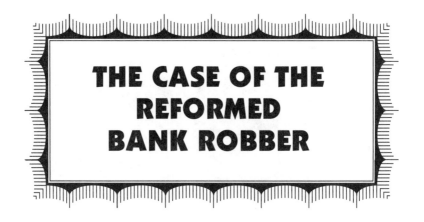

THE CASE OF THE REFORMED BANK ROBBER

Cal Q. Leiter and Becky Smart had just finished cleaning Chief Smart's office when the Chief burst into the room.

"Cal, I got a phone call from a parole officer named Bea Williams," said the Chief. "Evidently one of her — ah — clients is a suspect in a bank robbery that occurred yesterday afternoon in the town of Harrisonburg. I said we'd meet her at her Midville office in about ten minutes." He nodded in Becky's direction. "You can come along, too, Beck."

Cal grabbed his baseball cap and followed Becky and the Chief outside to the patrol car. "This robbery was reported on the news last night," Cal said as he slid into the back seat. "They said the robber made off with $50,000."

"Yes," the Chief said, adjusting his rear-view mirror. "And get this: Bea Williams' client specialized in robbing banks a few years back." The Chief pulled out into Main Street. "But I'm sure that's just a coincidence," he added sarcastically.

At Ms. Williams' office, Cal, Becky, and the Chief

found the parole officer waiting in her conference room. Beside her sat a muscular man wearing a loud plaid sports jacket.

"This is Casey Rockleford," said Ms. Williams, pointing to the muscular man. "Casey, this is Chief Smart."

"I'm innocent," snarled Casey. "Sure, I drove Ms. Williams up to Harrisonburg early yesterday afternoon, but I was back here in Midville when that robbery took place."

"Please tell us your story from the beginning, Mr. Rockleford," said the Chief.

Casey sprang from his chair and began pacing. "It's this simple," he said. "Ms. Williams and I left Midville in her car yesterday at 2:00 in the afternoon. And we pulled into Harrisonburg at 4:00. I dropped her off, turned around, and came directly home."

Ms. Williams nodded. "Yes, that's correct. Mr. Rockleford drove me to Harrisonburg and dropped me off to stay with my sister's family. I was planning to ride back with my mother — who has been with my sister's family for the past few days — next week, but when I heard about the trouble that Mr. Rockleford might be in, I had my mother drive me home this morning."

"Ms. Williams," said Cal, "are you sure about these departure and arrival times that Mr. Rockleford has given?"

"Positive," she replied.

Rockleford stopped pacing and pointed at the Chief. "I'm telling you, Chief, I did nothing wrong yesterday."

"How fast did you drive?" asked Cal.

"With Ms. Williams in the car, I had the cruise control set at 55 miles per hour for the entire way to Harrisonburg." Rockleford bit his lip. "On the way back, I gotta admit, I drove a little faster than that."

"He's right about the ride to Harrisonburg," said Ms. Williams, nodding. "He drove exactly at 55 mph. Of course, that car can't go much faster anyway. Before we left Midville, a mechanic told us we'd be lucky to get that old car up to 65 mph, because the transmission is starting to falter."

Cal began writing in his math notebook. "Did you spend any time in Harrisonburg, Mr. Rockleford?"

"Nope," he answered. "I dropped Ms. Williams off at the Harrisonburg exit ramp and got right back on the highway afterward. I didn't even go into the town."

"And you say that you were back here in Midville at

5:20, the time the bank robbery took place in Harrisonburg?" asked the Chief.

"Yesiree," said Rockleford confidently. "Look, I'm a reformed bank robber, not an active one. I have no desire to rob banks anymore."

"I don't suppose there's anyone here in Midville who can verify that you were here when the robbery was committed?" asked the Chief. "In other words, did anyone see you here in Midville at 5:20?"

Rockleford shook his head. "Nope, I went straight home to take a nap."

"Where do you live, Mr. Rockleford?" inquired Cal.

"Right next to the highway's off ramp, here in Midville."

Cal continued writing in his notebook. "So the entire round trip was spent driving on the highway?"

"Yes it was, kid." Rockleford's eyes narrowed. "What's that got to do with anything?"

Cal held up his notebook. "Chief, no one saw Mr. Rockleford in Midville at 5:20 because he wasn't within miles of here," said Cal. "His story simply isn't up to speed. I suggest you book him on suspicion of bank robbery."

How did Cal know that Casey Rockleford was lying about being back in Midville when the crime was committed? *(Solution on page 93.)*

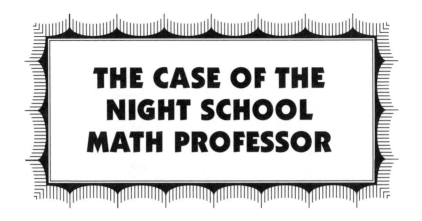

THE CASE OF THE NIGHT SCHOOL MATH PROFESSOR

"Wow, that was some finish," said 12-year-old junior detective Cal Q. Leiter. "I've never been to a game that went into triple overtime. Thank you for inviting me, Chief."

"You're certainly welcome, Cal. But it was Becky's idea to bring you along."

Cal blushed. "Thanks, Becky."

Becky smiled and nodded.

It was Saturday night and Cal, Chief Smart, and the Chief's daughter, Becky, were on their way home from the big game. Chief Smart had decided to take a short-cut through the Midville College campus. With the college closed for winter vacation, the Chief figured the campus would be empty and therefore it would take less time than driving through the center of town.

But as the three friends drove through the winding roads of the picturesque campus, Cal alertly spotted a light shining in one of the buildings.

"Chief," shouted Cal, pointing to the building. "Look, up there, on the third floor. Somebody is in there."

"So?" replied the Chief.

"I've taken a few math courses here, and that building is McFarland Hall, where they hold classes," said Cal. "Why would there be any classes on a Saturday night, during vacation?"

"Good point," answered the Chief as he pulled the car to a stop. "But I'm not prepared for trouble, so I better call in some backup, just in case."

After the Chief phoned officers Beth Belisle and Bernie McDermott, he motioned to Cal and Becky to follow him. The three friends dashed into the shadows and padded across the lawn to McFarland Hall's side entrance. There, they found the door smashed in. Leaping over the shattered glass, they entered the building and scrambled up two flights of stairs and down the hallway. When they reached the end of the hallway, they came to the classroom that was the source of the light.

The Chief opened the door, and Cal and Becky followed him into the room. "Hello there," said the Chief, flashing his badge.

"Hi, officer," said a man who was standing at the chalkboard.

"What's going on here?" asked the Chief.

The man at the chalkboard held up a piece of chalk. "I'm teaching a math class."

He pointed to a shaky-looking group of three men and a woman who were sitting at desks. "These folks are my — ah — students. My name is Smith. Ah, Professor Smith."

"You're teaching on a Saturday night?" asked Becky. "During vacation?"

"Yes, I am, little girl," he snapped. "These folks here are former high school dropouts who are trying to earn their high school equivalency degrees. They're here at night because they need some extra help."

Cal looked at the chalkboard and saw the following problems:

$2 + 6 \times 4$ divided by $2 =$

$18 - 2 + 3 \times 5 =$

Cal smiled. "I see you're showing your class some math problems," he said. "Don't let us stop you from teaching."

The Chief looked at Cal and frowned. "Cal, we don't have time to —"

"Sorry to interrupt you, Chief," Cal broke in. "But I think that it is very important to let the math professor teach his students how to solve these problems."

Smith turned to the chalkboard and went to work. "2 + 6 = 8; 8 × 4 is 32; and 32 divided by 2 equals 16." He wheeled around to face his students. "Any questions?"

The students answered, "No."

"Very well, then," said Smith. "Here's the next problem: 18 minus 2 is 16, + 3 is 19, × 5 = 95."

After Smith had finished the second problem, the Chief turned to Cal. "Well?"

"I don't know what this man is doing here," Cal said. "But he's clearly not a math teacher."

"That's good enough for me," bellowed the Chief. He then turned to officers Belisle and McDermott, who moments earlier had arrived at the scene. "Take this impostor and his cohorts downtown on suspicion of breaking and entering."

How did Cal know that Mr. Smith was not a math teacher? *(Solution on page 92.)*

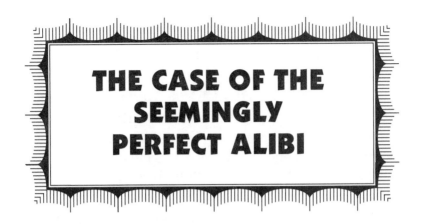

THE CASE OF THE SEEMINGLY PERFECT ALIBI

The loud roar of machinery made junior detective Cal Q. Leiter and Midville Police Chief Smart cover their ears as they trudged through the Fabulous Fabrics cloth factory. Everywhere they looked, the two friends saw huge mechanical devices that shook and shimmied and banged and clanged.

"Where's the owner's office?" shouted Cal.

The Chief pointed ahead. "Down there," he yelled, his voice almost lost in the ear-splitting noise that filled the building, "near that soda machine."

By the time Cal and Chief Smart reached the office, their ears were ringing. Eager to escape the blare of the thundering machinery, the Chief and Cal pounded on the office door. After a few seconds, the door opened and a lady appeared. Her name tag told Cal and the Chief that she was Ms. Farrington, one of the factory's co-owners. Following introductions, Ms. Farrington led the two detectives into the office.

"Please tell us what's been going on," said the Chief when everybody was seated.

"We've got a thief among us," said Ms. Farrington.

"A couple of watches were stolen from some employees' lockers this morning between 8:00 and 9:00."

"Any suspects?" asked the Chief.

"We thought we had one," answered Ms. Farrington. "A man named Lester Hackett. We found the stolen watches in his lunchbox, which he accidentally dropped on his way to the cafeteria. The lunch box broke open and the two watches fell out. "

The Chief looked puzzled. "Why is he no longer considered a suspect?"

"Because he has a reliable person who can provide him an alibi."

"We need to talk to that person," said Chief Smart sternly.

Ms. Farrington frowned. "You have been." She blushed a deep crimson. "I'm his alibi."

The Chief leaned forward. "This I gotta hear."

"Mr. Hackett is a new employee. He works in the cutting room. Today he was working all alone and we had only one machine working, so I went and watched him get started at precisely 8:00."

Cal broke in. "So you were with Mr. Hackett from 8:00 until 9:00?"

"Well, no," she answered. "I left after he got started, but I returned at exactly 9:00 to check in on him."

Again, the Chief looked confused. "How, then, are you his alibi? He had lots of time to leave the cutting room unnoticed."

"Let me explain: Mr. Hackett operates the cloth cutter. The machine does all of the work, but we need an operator to push the a button to get the machine to cut. Anyway, the machine makes one cut per minute. After each cut is completed, the operator pushes the

button to start the next cut." She stopped talking and took a deep breath. "Anyway, from 8:00 until 9:00, Mr. Hackett cut a 60-yard piece of cloth into 60 one-yard pieces. That's 60 cuts in 60 minutes. So that means Mr. Hackett could not possibly have left the cutting room during the hour."

"How far are the employee lockers from the cutting room?" asked Cal.

"Just across the hall; you can get there in 10 seconds."

The Chief made a sour face. "Cal, where are you going with this?" he said in an impatient voice. "Let's say it takes 10 seconds to get there, then 20 or 30 seconds to grab a couple of watches from the lockers, and another 10 seconds to return. That's almost one minute. Ms. Farrington said Mr. Hackett had cut 60 one-yard pieces of cloth in 60 minutes. Hackett had absolutely no time — not even a second — to spare."

Cal smiled. "But there's one small aspect of this situation you are not taking into consideration," he said. "Hackett did have time to commit this robbery; I can prove it."

What did Cal figure out that the Chief had missed? *(Solution on page 91.)*

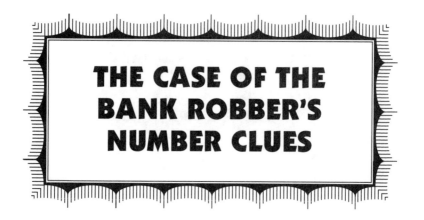

THE CASE OF THE BANK ROBBER'S NUMBER CLUES

Police Chief Arthur Smart and Cal Q. Leiter stood at the end of the dock, peering out across Deer Lake. They were on the lookout for Gary Herbertson, a big-time bank robber who had robbed the Midville Bank earlier that morning. Cal and the Chief had received an anonymous tip that Herbertson had rented a speedboat and was careening across Deer Lake toward a camp in Mallard Cove.

"Look!" yelled the Chief. "There's a boat that fits the description out there."

Cal squinted as he looked across the sparkling water. In the distance he could make out a bright red speedboat. "That sure looks like the one."

While Cal and the Chief watched, the speedboat disappeared around a bend in the lake. After putting on helmets, the two investigators hopped on four-wheel all-terrain vehicles and roared off toward the point where they had last seen the boat.

Minutes later, Cal and the Chief found the speedboat. It was beached in front of a shoreside log cabin.

There, they found Gary Herbertson, too. He was sprinting toward the cabin.

"Stop, Police," bellowed Chief Smart.

Herbertson threw up his hands and stopped in his tracks. "Sure, why not," he said. "I've done nuthin' wrong."

The Chief and Cal marched Gary Herbertson back to the speedboat. But despite searching the boat thoroughly, they found no money.

Herbertson laughed. "Money? What money? I've been out cruising the lake all day," he said with a smirk, when the Chief questioned him about the bank robbery.

"He's lying," said a voice from the nearby woods.

The Chief, Cal, and Gary Herbertson spun around

in time to see a tiny woman step out from behind a tree. She was dressed in a security guard's uniform.

"Who are you?" asked the Chief.

"My name is Linda Gold." She made her way over to where the boat was beached. "I'm a security guard at Midville Bank."

"How'd you get here?"

"After the bank was robbed, I received an anonymous phone call that the robber was going to rent a speedboat at Hardy's Marina," she said. "So I went to the marina and climbed into the boat's storage compartment while the suspect was paying the rental."

"So, you saw Herbertson with the money?" said the Chief.

"No," Linda Gold replied. "But while I was hiding on the boat I did hear him radio his wife to tell her where he hid the money."

"Terrific," yelled the Chief. "Where?"

"In a locker at Midville High School."

The Chief fished a notebook out of his coat pocket. "What's the number?"

Linda Gold shook her head. "Now that I don't know — not exactly, anyway."

"That's just great," said the Chief sarcastically. "There must be over 1000 lockers at Midville High."

Cal spoke up. "You said, 'not exactly,' Ms. Gold. What did you mean?"

"Well," said Linda, "the robber told his wife that he didn't dare to write the clues down on paper and that he didn't dare give her the number either. When the wife asked him how he would remember the locker number, he told her about the clues that he had used that would help him."

Cal smiled. "Can you recall those clues?" he asked.

"No problem," she said. "Being crammed in that storage compartment, there was nothing else to do but memorize the clues.

"First of all, he said that the locker number was a three-digit number, and that all three digits were either square or cube numbers. Next, he said that all three digits were different.

"He then told his wife that the digits were in order, least to greatest, and that the sum of the digits was less than 15."

Cal had been scribbling in his notebook furiously. He paused from writing and looked up. "Did he say anything else?"

"As a matter of fact, he did. He said that the product of the digits was less than 35."

Cal finished writing and thanked Linda Gold. He then turned to the Chief. "Here's the locker number, Chief. Mr. Herbertson's number clues clued us in."

The Chief grabbed Herbertson by the arm. "Come on Herbertson, we're going downtown."

What was the number of the locker, and how did Cal figure it out? *(Solution on p. 94.)*

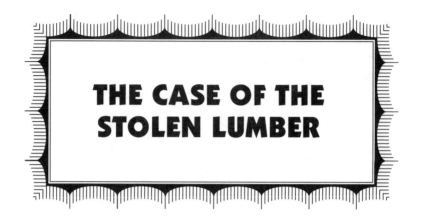

THE CASE OF THE STOLEN LUMBER

"I just got a phone call from Mayor Fuller," said Chief Smart. "Someone stole most of her new house."

Cal Q. Leiter's jaw dropped. "Pardon?"

"Come on," said the Chief. "We've got to get down there, pronto."

On the way to the crime scene, Chief Smart briefed Cal of the facts: Some time the day before, between 6 a.m. and 5 p.m., someone stole thousands of dollars' worth of lumber from the work site where the mayor's new home was to be built. The backhoe operator and the truck driver, the only two people who had been at the site that day, claimed the lumber must have been stolen late in the day, after they had taken their final load of dirt away. The two workers said they spent the entire day digging the hole for the foundation and hauling the dirt off to a gravel pit that was a mile away from the work site.

When Cal and the Chief arrived at the mayor's house lot, they found Mayor Linda Fuller and an elderly man standing near a large rectangular hole in the ground.

"Thank you for coming so quickly," said Mayor Fuller. She motioned to the elderly man. "This is Ernest Willowdale. He lives just down the road. I'm hoping he can help us."

After Cal and the Chief shook hands with Mr. Willowdale, the old man told his story. "I was out in front of my house all day, videotaping the squirrels and chipmunks that run about in my yard," he said. "I'm hoping to put together a documentary on these little creatures.

"But that darn dump truck, with all of its banging and clanging all day long, back and forth, ruined my documentary. I was so ticked off at how often that truck went by that I watched the tape last night, just to count how many trips were made. I was thinking that I might file a complaint with the town office, and I wanted to get my facts straight."

"And how many trips did you count?" asked Cal, notebook now in hand.

"They went back and forth 68 times," said Willowdale. "That's 34 loads of dirt they hauled away from here."

"Did you notice if the truck was full of dirt each trip?" asked Cal.

"Yes," the old man replied. "The dirt was level with the top on each and every trip."

"Well," said the Chief, "that eliminates the truck driver and backhoe operator as suspects."

Just then a dump truck rumbled onto the lot and screeched to a stop. Two workers — a tall crew-cut man and a short-bearded man — climbed out of the truck.

"That's them," croaked Willowdale. "Their names are Mac McNeely and Sully Sullivan."

McNeely and Sullivan told their story. It was the same story they had told Sergeant Belisle and Sergeant McDermott, the officers who earlier in the day had prepared a case fact sheet for the Chief.

"That's a nice truck there," said Cal to McNeely and Sullivan. "How much payload will it hold?"

McNeely smiled. "She'll hold eight cubic yards."

Cal wrote the numbers in his notebook: then he looked at the hole that the two workers had dug. "What are the dimensions?" he asked, pointing to the hole.

"It's 30 feet long by 24 feet wide by 9 feet deep," barked Sullivan.

Cal did some calculations as the Chief spoke with the mayor. "I'm sorry, Mayor," the Chief said, shaking his head sadly. "Looks like we really don't have any leads."

Cal held up his notebook. "Actually, Chief, we do. I think you need to take Mr. McNeely and Mr. Sullivan in for questioning."

What led Cal to suspect McNeely and Sullivan? *(Solution on page 91.)*

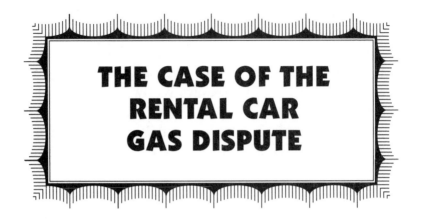

THE CASE OF THE RENTAL CAR GAS DISPUTE

It was 5:00 p.m. on a Friday afternoon. Chief Smart and Cal Q. Leiter were on their way to reserve a rental car for the Chief's nephew, Francis.

"What happened to your nephew's car?" asked Cal.

The Chief shook his head. "He drove it into the neighbor's swimming pool," answered the Chief. "He said he thought the pool was empty."

Cal's jaw dropped.

"Don't even ask," blurted the Chief. "You wouldn't believe me if I told you." The Chief swung the patrol car into the Quality Rental Car parking lot. As the car approached the office building, Cal saw three people arguing in the doorway.

Wayne O'Malley, the Quality Rental Car manager, was standing with a man who was wearing a tuxedo and a woman who was dressed in a bridal gown. All three people were screaming. The woman was shaking her fist at Mr. O'Malley, while the man kept pushing a piece of paper toward O'Malley's face.

After the Chief parked the police cruiser in front of

the argumentative trio, the two detectives hopped out to settle the matter.

"This is an outrage," growled the man in the tuxedo.

"Hey, what's going on here?" bellowed the Chief.

All three turned to the Chief and began shouting at the same time.

The Chief covered his ears and stood motionless. After a few seconds of absorbing the noise, he could take no more. "Enough, enough!" he roared. "There's no need to yell. Let's talk this over like civilized folks."

All three quieted down and nodded.

The Chief pointed to Mr. O'Malley. "Wayne, you go first."

"I rented a sports car to these newlyweds yesterday," he said, mopping the sweat from his forehead. "I had just washed and polished the vehicle."

Wayne paused to catch his breath. "The Quality Rental Car policy — and it's right in the contract they signed — states that renters must return the car with the same amount of gas as was in the tank when they left the lot." He pointed to the bride and groom. "In

their case, there was seven-eighths of a tank when they drove out of here."

The bride broke in. "So we forgot to put gas in. Big deal. We told him we'd pay him for it now. But we think he's done his math incorrectly."

"Yeah," said the groom through gritted teeth. "He's trying to rip us off by overcharging." He began jabbing his finger at Mr. O'Malley.

"O.K., O.K.," said Chief Smart. "Settle down, sir." The Chief turned to Cal. "Do you have any questions, Cal?"

"Mr. O'Malley," said Cal, "how much gas is in the tank now?"

"The gauge reads one-fourth full."

Cal jotted the figure in his notebook. "And how much does the tank hold in all?"

"Sixteen gallons," said O'Malley. He held up a car owner manual. "See, it says so right here."

The Chief snatched the manual from O'Malley and took a look. "Yup, he's right. Sixteen gallons."

"So, Mr. O'Malley," said Cal. "For how many gallons of gas did you charge these folks?"

"I charged them for eight gallons."

Wasting no time, Cal completed his calculations and handed his notebook to Chief Smart.

The Chief nodded.

Cal then turned to the newlyweds. "I have some good news and some bad news," he said. "The good news is you were right. Mr. O'Malley's math was wrong. The bad news is that he erred in your favor. You actually owe him for more than the eight gallons of gas that he had incorrectly figured."

How many gallons of gas did the newlyweds actually use? *(Solution on page 93).*

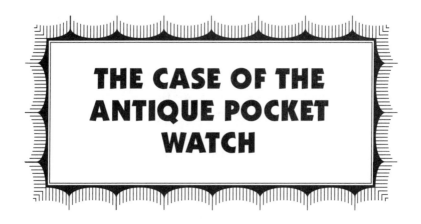

THE CASE OF THE ANTIQUE POCKET WATCH

Chief Smart and Cal Q. Leiter stared at millionaire Frederick Fillmore's valuable antique pocket watch. The broken watch possessed a tiny hole, the result of a bullet that had been fired at the eccentric old millionaire while he had slept in his bed earlier that afternoon. Ironically, the watch saved Fillmore's life. According to the police report, Fillmore customarily wore the watch like a necklace, and the priceless antique took the role of a shield, preventing the bullet from entering Fillmore's body.

As a result of the harrowing experience, Fillmore was in the hospital, suffering from shock. He was still unconscious.

While the Chief introduced himself to Fillmore's relatives, Cal took a closer look at the watch. The bullet had narrowly missed the watch's two hands, ending up lodged in the tiny interior gears. Since the timepiece stopped functioning upon the bullet's impact, the time that the hands showed, 2:02, gave the time of the attempted murder. Cal wrote this in his notebook.

After Chief Smart finished talking with Fillmore's

relatives, he turned to Mrs. Jeeves, Mr. Fillmore's maid. "Please tell us what you know, madam."

Mrs. Jeeves nodded. "Each and every afternoon, all six of Mr. Fillmore's relatives visit him. These days, Mr. Fillmore sleeps most of the time his relatives are with him, but that doesn't matter. They still visit anyway. The family insists that it's their way of showing they care." Mrs. Jeeves leaned toward the two detectives and whispered, "I think that all six were worried that old Mr. Fillmore was going to cut them out of his will."

"Did they visit at specific times?" asked Cal.

"Yes," replied Mrs. Jeeves. "Mr. Fillmore was a very regimented old man. He insisted on a set schedule. He said that all six could visit every day, but he wanted the visits short and always at the same times. Today, as usual, Cynthia was with Mr. Fillmore from 1:45 to 1:50; Julie was 1:50 to 1:55; Marge, 1:55 to 2:00; Don, 2:00 to 2:05; Jillian, 2:05 to 2:10; and Nick, 2:10 to 2:15."

The Chief wrote these figures in his notebook. Then he looked at the six relatives who were huddled in the corner of the room. They were bickering and pointing accusatory fingers at each other. "What did those folks have to say?" he asked Mrs. Jeeves.

"Each of them said that Mr. Fillmore appeared to be sleeping," said Mrs. Jeeves.

"Were they all on their regular schedules?" asked Cal.

"Yes," said Mrs. Jeeves. "I can attest to that. I let each one in. According to the old grandfather clock in the hall outside Mr. Fillmore's door, each relative was right on schedule. And that old clock keeps perfect time."

"Well," declared the Chief, "this is the easiest case we've ever had." He looked at Cal and smiled confi-

dently. "You see, I observed that the watch stopped precisely at 2:02. It's obvious that Mr. Fillmore was shot at 2:02 by —" he stopped to scan through his notes — "by Don. He must have used a silencer, so no one could hear the gunfire."

Mrs. Jeeves shook her head. "Not so fast, officer. It's not that simple. I'm sure you're correct about the silencer, because I never heard a sound, and I was just down the hall. But we have a slight problem as far as the time on that watch is concerned."

The Chief frowned. "How's that, Mrs. Jeeves?"

"You see, while Mr. Fillmore adored that watch, it did not keep good time. In fact, it lost eight minutes every 24 hours," she said. "So it wasn't showing the same time — the real time — as the old grandfather clock I was going by when I sent each person into the old man's room."

The Chief's shoulders drooped. "Darn. I guess this is not an open-and-shut case."

"Is there anything else you can tell us that might help, Mrs. Jeeves?" said Cal.

Mrs. Jeeves nodded. "Yes," she said, "there certainly is. You see, I would set the watch correct each night at 11 p.m. before I left this house to go home to my apartment."

Cal resumed working in his notebook and, after a few minutes, he finished his calculations. "I know who shot Mr. Fillmore," he said. "It's time to reveal the culprit."

Who shot Mr. Fillmore? *(Solution on page 94.)*

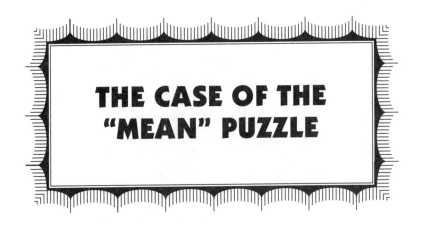

THE CASE OF THE "MEAN" PUZZLE

"Yup. That Mean Sam Keene was the best pro football player I've ever seen," said Midville's veteran Police Chief Arthur Smart. "And he certainly took his nickname to an extreme level."

Twelve-year-old Cal Q. Leiter looked up from his advanced calculus book.

"How's that, Chief?"

"Everything was *mean* this and *mean* that," replied the Chief. "His sports car was the Meanmobile. His restaurant was named Mean Eats. The shoes he endorsed were called Mean Boots. His sports drink was Mean Keenade. His —"

"I get your point, Chief," Cal cut in. "The man liked everything mean."

The Chief turned the squad car into a driveway that led up to a fancy single-story brick house situated on a sprawling estate. "Here we are," said the Chief. "Mean Sam Keene's house. Well, it used to be his house. In his will, he left it to his brother."

After the Chief parked the car, the two detectives went to the front door and gave the bell a ring. A sec-

ond later, the door opened and a middle-aged woman stood in front of them.

The Chief smiled. "Howdy, I'm Police Chief Smart," he said, flashing his badge. "This young fella is my assistant, Calvin Quincy Leiter."

The woman introduced herself as Josephine Keene, Mean Sam's sister. "Here's the situation, gentlemen," she began. "As you may know, Samuel had a few quirks. One of these quirks was his fondness for making up puzzles and having other people solve them."

The Chief scratched his head. "That's nice, Ms. Keene, but what's that got to do with you calling us?"

"Well, Chief," Ms. Keene said, her face red, "if you would let me finish, you'd find out. Anyway, Samuel left this house to my brother. He left me a $1 million ring. But here's the catch: prankster that he was, Samuel hid the ring somewhere in this house."

The Chief looked around the house. "Wow, where do we begin?"

"We don't," replied Ms. Keene. "Although this isn't a large house: kitchen, dining room, den, one bedroom, one bath, and a full basement, we shouldn't tear apart a $2 million house to find a $1 million ring. And besides, it's not my house."

The Chief frowned. "Yes, but —"

"If you can solve this puzzle, we won't need to do any demolition," Ms. Keene said, reaching into her purse.

She fished out a sheet of paper. "This was in Samuel's safety deposit box," she said. "It tells where he hid the ring, but it's in some sort of a code. Crack the code, and I'll make a generous donation to our town."

Ms. Keene handed the paper to the Chief, who in turn handed it to Cal. On the paper Cal saw groups of numbers and letters inside rectangles. (We've printed them on the next page.) Cal studied the paper as Ms. Keene spoke.

"I thought I had found a couple of patterns," she explained. "But neither one led to anything that made sense." She looked at Cal and frowned. "Doesn't he need a calculator or something?"

The Chief laughed. "Not this kid, ma'am. He *is* a calculator. Seriously, this kid is a certified genius."

Cal pulled out a notebook and began working. After a couple of minutes, he smiled and held out his notebook.

Before he could say anything, the Chief snatched the notebook out of Cal's hands. The Chief looked at the notebook and shook his head. "Well, I'll be. You've done it again, Cal. It looks like the town will be getting a nice donation, thanks to you."

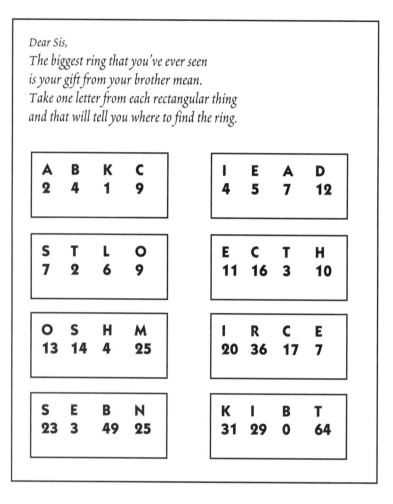

Dear Sis,

The biggest ring that you've ever seen
is your gift from your brother mean.
Take one letter from each rectangular thing
and that will tell you where to find the ring.

A	B	K	C
2	4	1	9

I	E	A	D
4	5	7	12

S	T	L	O
7	2	6	9

E	C	T	H
11	16	3	10

O	S	H	M
13	14	4	25

I	R	C	E
20	36	17	7

S	E	B	N
23	3	49	25

K	I	B	T
31	29	0	64

Cal laughed. "Maybe a new police chief's office is in the future, huh, Chief?"

Where is the ring hidden? What pattern did Cal discover? What did Mean Sam's puzzle mean? Why is this just an average puzzle? Hint: You may want to look up the word *mean* in the dictionary. *(Solution on page 87.)*

THE CASE OF THE WORRIED LOTTERY WINNER

A steady rain pounded the patrol car windshield as Chief Arthur Smart and his 12-year-old passenger, Cal Q. Leiter, skidded into the Midville Savings Bank parking lot. "It's really coming down now," shouted Cal over the crackle of thunder. "I know we've all been wishing for rain, but this is a bit much."

The Chief did not respond. He was too busy looking for the girl who had phoned in the request for assistance. The girl had insisted that it wasn't an emergency, but she had been adamant that she needed immediate help.

"Over there," said the Chief, pointing to the bank entry door. Cal turned his head and spotted a teenage girl in a bright yellow raincoat waving an umbrella. The Chief pulled up to where the girl was standing. When the two detectives got out of the car, she rushed toward them. Besides the umbrella, she also was holding a cellular phone.

"Thank you for answering my call so quickly," the girl said.

The Chief started towards the bank door. "I'm Chief

Smart," he said. "And this is my partner, Calvin
Leiter. Can we talk inside?"

"No, no." The girl grabbed the Chief's arm. "My
aunt is in there. And she's the reason I'm guarding
the door. We can't let her hear what we're talking
about. I'll feel like such a fool if I'm wrong."

The girl held the umbrella over the Chief and Cal.
"Here, we can all stay dry," she said.

"Very well then, young lady, we'll stay outside." The Chief sneezed. "Now tell us what's going on here."

"My name is Christina Markus," the girl said. "And I think my aunt — she's also my legal guardian — is trying to cheat me out of a lot of money. You see, each week I give her a dollar to buy me a lottery ticket. That's because I'm not old enough to buy a ticket myself. And —"

"Let me guess," the Chief interrupted. "You won."

Christina Markus beamed. "As a matter of fact, I did. It's still hard for me to believe, but I won $300,000; that's $240,000 after taxes."

The Chief whistled. "Wow."

"Congratulations," Cal said.

The girl nodded sheepishly. "Anyway, my aunt said that she should get a little bit of the money, since she was the one who actually purchased the ticket. Naturally, I agreed. She said that we should keep one-fourth of it in cash for the two of us to share and that we should put the rest into a long-term savings account for me to get at when I'm 18."

Cal took out his math notebook and began jotting down numbers.

"She then said that her share would be one-fifth of the cash we were getting and that the rest of the cash would be mine," Christina said. "She told me she would send me my share after she takes a trip to Europe."

"Sounds like your aunt is being fair," the Chief said.

"Yes," said Christina. "That's what I thought, too. So I agreed to her proposal."

"How much did your aunt figure she should get?" asked Cal.

Christina took a piece of paper from her coat pocket. "That's where I have my concerns. Here are my aunt's figures: one-fifth plus one-fourth equals nine-twentieths. And nine-twentieths of $240,000 is $108,000." She showed the paper to Cal. "I checked her work on a calculator, and it all checks out. One-fifth plus one-fourth does equal nine-twentieths, and nine-twentieths of $240,000 is $108,000. But somehow it just doesn't seem right."

The Chief shrugged his shoulders and turned to Cal, who was busy writing.

Cal looked up from his notebook and smiled. "It was smart of you to call us, Ms. Markus," he said. He then handed the Chief his notebook. "Do you see what went on here, Chief?"

The Chief looked at Cal's work and nodded. "Cal, we can always bank on you to solve the case."

Can you see what went on? How was Christina being cheated by her aunt? What did Cal notice about the aunt's math? *(Solution on page 89.)*

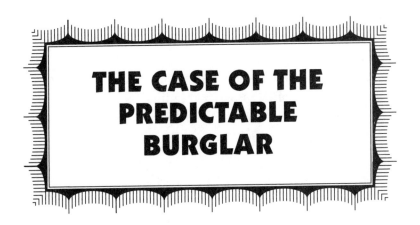

THE CASE OF THE PREDICTABLE BURGLAR

Joyce Thomas, owner of the Portland Owls profession-
al football team, frowned as she hung up the tele-
phone. "That was our coach, Kenny Hutchinson,"
Thomas said to Midville Police Chief Arthur Smart
and his 12-year-old sidekick, Cal Q. Leiter. "Coach
says the burglar hit two more players' homes yesterday afternoon during the game against the Bengals."

"That's the fifth Sunday in a row," said the Chief.
"Any clues this time?"

"Just the usual. The burglar left a note saying he
would burgle two more players during next week's
game. And he dared us to figure out which two."

"Confident fellow, isn't he," said Cal.

"Yes, he is," said the Chief.

"Have you noticed any patterns to the crimes,
Ms. Thomas?" asked Cal, as he opened up his math
notebook.

"Well," said Ms. Thomas, "the Portland police
department thought they had found a pattern, but as
it turned out, it was nothing." She paused. "That's
why we called you guys. We've heard wonderful things

about the way you solve crimes up there in that little town of yours."

The Chief beamed.

"Just out of curiosity," said Cal, "what was it that caught the eye of the Portland police?"

"It had something to do with the players' jersey numbers," answered Ms. Thomas. "Come over to my desk calendar and I'll show you."

Cal and the Chief followed Ms. Thomas to her desk. On the calendar, Cal saw five dates circled and in each circle were two numbers: November 2 (3 & 5); November 9 (5 & 7); November 16 (11 & 13); November 23 (17 & 19); and November 30 (29 & 31).

Cal studied the calendar as the Chief and Ms. Thomas resumed their conversation.

"The Portland cops looked for all sorts of patterns, and the closest thing they could find was the fact that the jersey numbers of the two players robbed each week were two away from each other. The numbers in the circles are the burgled players' numbers." Ms. Thomas shook her head sadly. "Poor Anderson, our place kicker, got robbed twice. He's #5."

"And?" inquired the Chief.

"And that's where it stopped," said Thomas. "Having #5 show up twice botched up any kind of pattern we thought we had found. Besides, we have 60 players on this football team, with numbers ranging from 1 to 99. There are numerous possibilities where we have a difference of two between two players' numbers. How are we — or the cops — supposed to figure out which two players will be hit next?"

The Chief sighed. "Yes, it's too bad we don't have a pattern here."

Hoping to find some sort of clue, Cal sat down and reached into his backpack. He pulled out a notebook and a box of pens. Next, he wrote the numbers 1 through 99 on the paper and circled the numbers of the players who had been robbed so far. Cal studied the list in front of him for several minutes, looking for a pattern. Then he said, "Actually, we do have a pattern." He circled two additional numbers and showed them to Ms. Thomas. "Are there any players on your team who wear these numbers?"

Ms. Thomas grabbed a team photograph from the top drawer of her desk. "Yes, yes," she said joyously.

"Then these are the two players who the burglar plans to rob next Sunday," Cal said.

Who will the burglar rob next Sunday? How did Cal come to that conclusion? *(Solution on page 91.)*

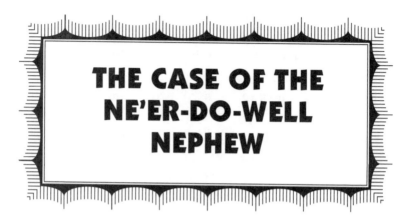

THE CASE OF THE NE'ER-DO-WELL NEPHEW

Cal Q. Leiter looked at the store sign and wrinkled his forehead. "Ye Olde Coin and Stamp Shop," he read. "Why are we stopping here?" he asked Chief Smart. "Has there been a crime committed?"

Chief Smart shook his head. "No, my young friend. No crime. I'm just here to visit my nephew, Francis. He's kind of a goofy kid, what you might call a ne'er-do-well, and my brother asked me to check in on him."

The Chief opened the store's door, and overhead a small bell jingled. Cal followed the Chief into the shop and looked around. The shop was empty of people, and it was a mess. Papers, folders, books, and boxes littered the floor.

"Looks like a cyclone hit this place," Cal said.

The Chief shook his head. "Looks like Francis's work to me."

Just then a pimply-faced clerk in his twenties popped up from behind the counter. "Uncle Art, am I glad to see you!" he said. "Maybe you can help me. I've messed up again."

"What is it this time, Francis?"

After the Chief introduced Cal to his nephew, the

frazzled clerk told his story. "I've worked here for three weeks, and I haven't made a single sale yet. My boss says that if I don't sell anything by tomorrow, I'm fired. I don't want to be fired, Uncle Art. I like this job."

"Okay, Francis. How can we help you?"

"This morning, a customer came into the store and said he'd like to buy one of these special edition 1976 Liberty Bell stamps." Francis held up a clear plastic binder sleeve that housed a dozen or so stamps that featured the Liberty Bell. "The problem is that I don't know how much my boss wants me to charge for this particular stamp. That's because I lost the individual stamp price guide list he gave me."

The Chief frowned. "Oh, Francis."

"I know, I know," he said glumly. "I've been searching the store for the past two hours, but it hasn't turned up anywhere. And the customer is due back within the hour."

"Why don't you call your boss?" asked the Chief.

"No can do," Francis replied. "He's on vacation. And he told me not to disturb him. If I call him, he'll fire me for sure."

At this point, Cal noticed a chalkboard on the wall that said: "Stamp Collectors' Specials of the Week: one 1976 Liberty Bell plus one 1976 George Washington for $140; one 1976 Liberty Bell plus one 1981 Elvis commemorative for $77; and one 1976 George Washington and one 1981 Elvis commemorative for $105."

Francis observed Cal looking at the chalkboard. "That doesn't help us any," said Francis. "It doesn't show individual prices."

The Chief nodded. "He's right, Cal. Math isn't going to help us here. We've got to find that price guide by getting our hands dirty. We're going to have to turn this place even more upside down that it is already."

While the Chief and Francis began tearing through shelves and file cabinets, Cal took out his math notebook and started calculating.

"Cal!" shouted the Chief. "Aren't you going to help us look?"

Cal looked up from his notebook. "There's no need to look," he said. "I can tell you the price of the Liberty Bell stamp."

"How's that?" asked the Chief and Francis in unison.

Cal grinned. "The sign said it all."

What is the Liberty Bell stamp's price? How did Cal use the information on the sign to determine the price. *(Solution on page 92.)*

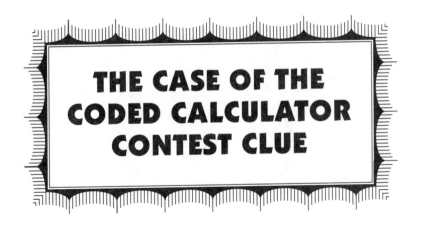

THE CASE OF THE CODED CALCULATOR CONTEST CLUE

"The birdhouse near the garden!" shouted Becky Smart. "The final clue is in the birdhouse near the garden!" Police Chief Smart's 12-year-old daughter began jumping up and down. "We've done it, Cal. Quickly, let's get to that birdhouse."

Becky started racing up the brick walkway that led to the garden, and her friend, junior detective Cal Q. Leiter, sprinted along behind her.

As the two ran along, Cal thought about the chain of events that had led to this exciting moment. One week earlier, Becky had won the annual Hugo G. Rensberger Essay Contest. In addition to winning $50 worth of mystery books, Becky had the opportunity to visit the Rensberger Estate to try to solve a series of puzzles which led to a grand prize of $500 in gold. She was allowed to bring one friend, and she chose Cal.

In the ten years in which the best-selling mystery author Rensberger had run this contest, no one had ever won the grand prize. But Becky thought that with two great minds — hers and Cal's — their chances of winning the gold would be very good. Now,

at the beautiful Rensberger Estate, Becky and Cal had just that chance. They had solved the ninth of ten puzzles, and they were one question away from finding the hidden gold.

They had not run far when they passed the picturesque little pond that had caught Cal's attention an hour earlier when they had been looking for the sixth clue. Cal remembered the dock that stretched all the way to the pond's center, the big bell that hung from a granite post where the dock began, the bright yellow lampposts that dotted the dock's side, and the miniature lighthouse that stood in the middle of the pond.

Soon, they left the pond behind and came to the base of a steep hill. Without saying a word, the two friends started upward. Higher and higher they ran. The higher they went, the more tired they became. The hill had not seemed quite so steep when they had traveled this way previously.

Upon reaching the top, Becky grabbed Cal's coat sleeve. "Tired?"

Cal nodded, too tired to reply.

Finally, out of breath, they stopped. Exhausted, they plopped down on a granite bench to rest. Cal looked around. There was much to see at the top of the hill. On the left was a towering oak tree that held a fancy red cedar treehouse. To the right, Cal noticed another one of those big bells, exactly like the one at the pond. Behind the big bell was an old wishing well, and next to the well were two smaller bells.

Cal looked at Becky. "Ready?"

Becky nodded.

Encouraged by the fact that it was all downhill from there, Becky and Cal ran faster and harder. Soon, the brick walkway gave way to a dirt path. The path took Cal and Becky through a mazelike clump of shrubs, and when the two friends emerged, they found themselves standing at the edge of the garden. They climbed over a stone wall and stumbled into some roses. About 30 feet from where they were sitting, they saw the birdhouse that harbored the final clue.

They jumped to their feet and took off, running. They ran past a brick garden shed, past a marble statue of a scarecrow, and past a wheelbarrow full of bricks. At last, they got to the birdhouse.

Becky reached inside the little door and removed an envelope. With trembling hands she tore open the envelope and read the clue aloud. "Congratulations! You've made it to the final clue. To find the gold, solve these three math problems. The answers will tell you where the gold is hidden. Don't be too proud and vain; use a calculator to assist you."

"Must be difficult problems," said Cal, and he fished a calculator from his backpack. "O.K. Fire away."

Becky continued to read. "Problem number one: 410 plus 508. Problem number two: 5000 plus 2738. Problem number three: 6500 plus 1214."

Cal tossed the calculator back into the backpack and chuckled. "We don't need a calculator. These problems are simple. Here are the answers: 918, 7738, and 7714."

"But what do these numbers mean?" asked Becky.

Cal thought for a few moments and then shrugged. "I don't know," he said, shaking his head. "I don't know."

For a couple of minutes, neither Cal nor Becky said a word. They just stood there thinking.

Finally, Becky said, "Cal, the clue said, 'Don't be too proud or vain; use a calculator to assist you.' Go ahead and try again, using your calculator this time."

Cal retrieved the calculator from the backpack.

He tried each of the three problems again. Upon finishing the third one he laughed. "I obviously got the same answers as before," he said. "But now I know why the clue said to use a calculator. On a calculator the clues DO tell us where the gold is hidden."

What did the calculator's answers tell Cal? Where was the gold hidden? *(Solution on page 94.)*

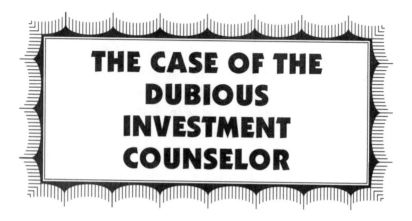

THE CASE OF THE DUBIOUS INVESTMENT COUNSELOR

Midville's junior math detective Cal Q. Leiter yawned and rubbed his eyes in an attempt to wake up. It was 11:30 p.m. and, along with Chief Smart, two uniformed police officers, and two men in business suits, Cal was sitting at an oval table in an office at the Greeley Investments Building in downtown Midville.

Sergeant Beth Belisle, the officer who had phoned the Chief, spoke first. "Officer McDermott and I were on regular patrol when we passed this building and noticed the lights were on. We rushed inside and caught these two guys rifling through the vault over there. They were stuffing $100 bills into a briefcase."

The Chief smiled. "Well, I'm sure they can show us proper ID."

"No, sir, they can't," replied Officer Belisle. She then pointed a finger at the older of the two men in business suits, a bald man who sat beside Cal. "This gentleman says he's Joseph Greeley, owner and chief investment counselor of Greeley Investments. He says he was paying off stock dividends to the other gentleman, a Mr. Jones."

Mr. Jones, sweating like a pig, nodded.

"Did they say anything besides that?" asked Cal.

Officer Belisle shook her head. "Not a thing."

The Chief looked at Officer Belisle, then at Cal. "I've never stepped foot in this building before tonight, nor have I ever met anyone who works at this company. I do know that the mayor, on the other hand, has served on various committees with Joseph Greeley. I hate to bother the mayor at this time of night, but we may have to get her down here to see whether this is indeed the real Mr. Joseph Greeley or an impostor and a criminal."

The man who claimed to be Joseph Greeley gave the Chief a nervous glance and said, "Look, it's late and I have to —"

"Let's hear your story, Greeley — or whoever you are," said the Chief abruptly.

"Well, sir, we were simply conducting a business transaction. I was paying Mr. Jones the money he had earned from a shrewd business tip I had given him."

"And what might that have been?" asked Cal.

"Potatoes, young man. Potatoes." Greeley smiled and leaned back in his chair. "You see, a company up-country discovered a way to cultivate huge potatoes, absolutely humungous I tell you, and I steered Mr. Jones toward investing with this outfit. Thanks to me, Mr. Jones made a tidy profit. The stocks of this potato company skyrocketed, and Mr. Jones asked me to sell his shares. I did as I was asked, of course, and that's why I'm now here, doling out all of this wonderful money. Mr. Jones insisted on cash."

"Do you normally do business this late at night?" asked the Chief.

Greeley shook his head. "No, Chief, normally I do

not. But Mr. Jones here called me about an hour ago and said that he absolutely, positively must have the money tonight since he was leaving town tomorrow morning before business hours. He was very firm about this. What could I do but accommodate him? You know the old saying: *The customer is always right.*"

"Would you mind telling us the details of Mr. Jones's investment?" asked Cal.

"Ah, ahem, ah — sure thing," replied Greeley. "He invested $15,000 and, with my help, he brought in $30,000."

Cal jotted the information down in his notebook. "Wow, that's a nice increase. What's that figure out to for a percent of increase?"

"You aren't much of a math student, young man. An increase from $15,000 to $30,000 is a piece of cake to figure: $30,000 is double $15,000, so it's a 200% increase."

The Chief scratched his head. "This is getting us nowhere fast. I still don't know if this man is Joseph Greeley or not. I guess we'll call the mayor and ask her to come on over to ID this gentleman here." He frowned. "She's not going to be happy, us waking her up in the middle of the night and all."

Cal stepped forward. "Chief, don't bother waking the mayor. This man is not Joseph Greeley. He's an impostor. And I can prove it."

Why was Cal so sure that the man was an impostor? *(Solution on page 89.)*

The Chief's Old Partner (page 16). When Cal did the math, he came upon a huge flaw. Judkins said that he started on the ground floor, which on a vertical number line would be considered zero. (The floors numbered 1 to 15 would be considered positive numbers on the number line, while the basement floor would be considered negative one, –1). When Cal added the numbers that Judkins had written in his tally worksheet, he at one point calculated a –2. That, of course, would be impossible, since the basement (–1) is the lowest floor in this building. Therefore, it proves that Judkins wrote these numbers in without actually having operated the elevator. There are other numbers that were impossible too.

The "Mean" Puzzle (page 65). The word "mean" has several definitions. The mathematical definition of mean is: The answer you get when the sum of the numbers in a set of data is divided by the number of pieces of data. In other words, when you find the mean in math, you are finding the average number of a set of data.

After you find the mean (average) of the 4 numbers of each rectangular box, take the letter that corresponds with the mean within that box. For example, in the first box, the mean of 2, 4, 1, and 9 (16 divided by 4) is 4. The letter B is above the 4. So the letter B is the answer for that box. When you have completed each box, you'll find that the eight letters spell BATH SINK. Therefore, the ring is hidden in the bathroom sink.

Hit-and-Run Taxi (page 12). Given the facts, Cal organized the information as follows: Bill on receipt minus driver's initial rate = charge for additional miles.

Freddy's	Smalltown	ASAP
$3.90	$3.90	$3.90
–1.00	–1.10	–.50
$2.90	$2.80	$3.40

3.3 miles minus driver's initial rate distance = the miles driven after the initial rate distance:

3.3	3.3	3.3
–.5	–.5	–.2
2.8	2.8	3.1

Since each taxi charged $.10 for each additional .1 mile (a 1 to 1 ratio) after the initial rate part of the ride, the amount charged for the additional part of the trip and the mileage driven for the additional part of the trip will match up for the guilty driver. Therefore, looking at the work above, the numbers show that Smalltown Taxi — Mary Jill Haverhill — was the attacker.

Carnival Probability (page 5). The probability of tossing three coins and getting two heads is the same as tossing three coins and getting one head. In both cases, the probability is 3 out of 8. Therefore, to make the money aspect of the game fair, it should be $2 to play with a $4 prize ($2 profit), *not* a $3 prize ($1 profit) when the customer wins. With the dishonest way the vendor has the game set up, he has a sure money-winner of a game for himself.

Dubious Investment Counselor (page 84). The man's math was incorrect. An increase from $15,000 to $30,000 is an increase of 100%, *not* 200%. Cal knew that a real investment counselor would have known that.

Mayor's Red Office (page 9). The least common multiple of 2 and 6 is 6. Together, it took Sue and Harry 2 hours to do one room, so that means that together they could do 3 rooms in 6 hours. Alone, Sue can do one room in 6 hours. Therefore, subtract 3 minus 1 to get 2 and that proves that Harry alone can do two rooms in 6 hours or 1 room in 3 hours. He had enough time to paint the room and drive over to the mayor's place, vandalize her office, and drive back to the hotel by 11:15.

Worried Lottery Winner (page 69). The aunt was *adding* $1/5$ plus $1/4$ and getting an answer of $9/20$. To find $1/5$ of $1/4$, the correct operation is multiplication, not addition: $1/5 \times 1/4 = 1/20$. And $1/20$ of $240,000 is $12,000.

Pizza Decision (page 32). Answer: A pizza is a circle. To figure out the area of a circle you must square the radius (multiply the radius by itself) and multiply that answer by pi (3.14). (Remember, a radius is half the size of a diameter.) So the area of a small pizza is 6 × 6 × 3.14 or 113 square inches, while the area of the large pizza is 12 × 12 × 3.14, or 452.16 square inches. Therefore, the area of four small pizzas is found by multiplying 113 × 4, which equals 452 square inches, the same area as one large pizza. Since four small pizzas cost $22 (4 times $5.50) and one large pizza costs $11, you figure $22 minus $11, or $11 is saved by buying one large instead of 4 small.

Fractured Will (page 21). $4,800,000. Here's how Cal figured this one out: Montgomery ended up with $800,000 after Edward had received one-third of what had remained. That means that $800,000 represents two-thirds of the remaining number before Edward received his cut. That means that there was $1,200,000 left before Edward got his money. So, that means that there was $1,200,000 after Jonathon got his cut of the money. Therefore, since Jonathon got one-half, there must have been double $1,200,00 or $2,400,000 available monies prior to Jonathon's receiving his cut. Since Henry got one-half of the original money, double $2,400,000 to find the original amount of money ($4,800,000) that Gertrude had left to the four nephews.

Fishy Alibi (page 35). All three guys left the wharf at 8 a.m. Paddy took 3 hours each round trip, Malcolm took 6 hours, and Frank 4 hours. When you count by threes, fours, and sixes, the lowest number in common is 12. That means 12 hours after they all began, or 8 p.m., is the first time that all three would retun to the wharf at the same time. The only one who was at the wharf at 4 p.m. was Frank. The other two were still out on the water at 4:00 p.m.

Predictable Burglar (page 73). The players who wear 41 and 43 were next on the burglar's list. Cal noticed that the players who were robbed so far wore numbers that were twin primes (prime numbers that differ by two) in the order that they occur in the list of counting numbers (3 & 5; 5 & 7; 11 & 13; 17 & 19; 29 & 31). The next pair of twin prime numbers are 41 and 43. So next Sunday the players who wear these numbers are the targets.

Seemingly Perfect Alibi (page 47). To get 60 pieces, only 59 cuts are necessary. When Hackett made the 59th cut, the result was the second to last piece *and* the last piece with that single cut. So he did have one minute of extra time to steal the watches.

Stolen Lumber (page 54) The hole was $30 \times 24 \times 9$ feet. That's 10 yards × 8 yards × 3 yards, or a total of 240 cubic yards. Since the dump truck holds 8 cubic yards, 240 divided by 8, or 30, is the number of trips needed to remove the dirt. But the workers made 34 trips, four more than needed. Old Mr. Willowdale said that he observed that each of the workers' loads had dirt level with the top of the truck's payload. For those four extra trips, McNeely and Sullivan were really carrying lumber with a skim coat of dirt on top to hide the stolen goods.

Night School Math Professor (page 43). When doing the two math problems, the man neglected to use the mathematical order of operations, in which, if there are no parentheses dictating otherwise, multiplying and dividing are always done before adding and subtracting. This is basic math that any real math teacher would have known. If you correctly follow the order of operations, the answer to the first problem is 14, not 16; and the answer to the second problem is 31, not 95.

Ne'er-Do-Well Nephew (page 76). Cal added $140 plus $77 to get the price for two Liberty Bells, one George Washington, and one Elvis. $140 + $77 = $217. Then he subtracted $105 (value of one George Washington and one Elvis) from $217 to leave him with $112. The difference of $112 is how much it cost for two Liberty Bells. To find the price for one Liberty Bell, divide $112 by 2. The answer is: one Liberty Bell costs $56.

Carpet Dealer (page 25). Although the Chief's math was correct, Cal's picture proved that Shady Sadee was lying. The combined areas of the five carpets *was* less than the area of the warehouse. But when Cal drew a picture, it was clear that all five of the unrolled, stretched-out carpets could not fit on the warehouse floor without overlapping. (Try this by drawing a picture.)

Missing Country Club Funds (page 29). When Cal added the five fractions $1/4 + 1/5 + 1/20 + 1/18 + 3/10$, he got a sum of $154/180$, or $77/90$. Cal realized that the five fractional parts *should* add up to one whole. That means that $1 - 77/90$, or $13/90$ of whatever had been in the treasury fund was missing.

Rental Car Gas Dispute: (page 58). 10 gallons. To find the answer, Cal started with $7/8$ and took away $1/4$ to get $5/8$. He then multiplied $5/8$ times 16 (total gallons the car holds) to get 10 gallons. Or: If the tank holds 16 gallons, $7/8$ is 14 gallons. If they returned with a tank $1/4$ full they had 4 gallons. $14 - 4 = 10$ gallons.

Reformed Bank Robber (page 39). Mr. Rockleford drove the car exactly at 55 mph on the way to Harrisonburg, and this trip took exactly two hours; the distance of the trip was 110 miles. To leave Harrisonburg at 4:00 and to be back in Midville at 5:20, Mr. Rockleford would have had to drive at about 83 mph (110 miles divided by $1 1/3$ hours). But this would be impossible, as the mechanic said the car would be lucky to reach 65 mph; therefore, Mr. Rockleford could not have been back home in Midville at 5:20.

Antique Pocket Watch (page 61). The culprit was Jillian. Since the watch lost 8 minutes every 24 hours, Cal estimated it lost one minute every 3 hours. The watch was set at 11 p.m., so at 2 a.m. it had lost 1 minute and it showed 1:59. At 5 a.m. it had lost 2 minutes and showed 4:58. At 8 a.m. it had lost 3 minutes and showed 7:57. At 11 a.m., it had lost 4 minutes and showed 10:56. At 2 p.m., it had lost 5 minutes and it showed 1:55. Since 2:02 is just two minutes after 2:00, the watch had not yet lost any additional time, so it was still 5 minutes behind the real time. Thus it was actually 2:07 when the shot was fired, and at 2:07 Jillian was in the room.

Coded Calculator Clue (page 79). The answer to the first problem is 918. When the number 918 shows up on a calculator and the calculator is turned upside down, it spells the word BIG. The answer to the second problem is 7738. When the number 7738 shows up on a calculator and the calculator is turned upside down, it spells the word BELL. When the number 7714 shows up on a calculator, it spells the word HILL. Therefore, the gold is hidden in the BIG BELL on the HILL.

Bank Robber's Number Clues (page 50). The locker was #148. The possible cubes are 1 and 8. The possible squares are 1, 4, and 9. The robber also said that all three digits were different, were in numerical order, and that the sum of the digits was less than 15. The number could have been 148 or 149. Finally, the robber said that the product of the digits was less than 35, and since $1 \times 4 \times 9 = 36$ and $1 \times 4 \times 8 = 32$, it is clear that the locker number must be 148.

INDEX